you have a
message you were
born to contribute!
xo
Ashley

Testimonies for Ashley

"There are not many publicists or publicity people as savvy as Ashley Crouch."
-Ali Brown, award-winning business coach

"We had super high demands that we wanted to accomplish in a really short period of time. We wanted television spots, sponsorships, radio spots, magazine placements, and Ashley delivered A-Z, providing the support, strategy, and pitches where needed. Ashley delivered beyond expectation and it was worth the investment times a thousand!!"

-Kelly Roach, international bestselling author

"Ashley is just the kind of advisor you want on your team. She truly knows how to build a following and make a lasting impression in media. It is clear why so many leaders choose her as their PR and Branding Consultant." **-Erica Dhawan, co-author of bestselling book *Get Big Things Done: The Power of Connectional Intelligence***

"Ashley Crouch is a powerful advocate for big ideas and thought-leaders. She inherently knows how to leverage and amplify a story so that it reaches the people who need it the most."

-Ann Shoket, former Editor-in-Chief of *Seventeen* Magazine

"Ashley is the real deal. She generously gives her knowledge and passion to benefit people who need to get their story told, but who are struggling to find the way to do so in an effective manner. Ashley's practical tips and advice work. It's that simple."

— **Adrienne Garland, Founder of She Leads Media**

"Ashley is great at her job. She works hard for her clients and makes the journalist's job a breeze. She gets things done."

– Elizabeth Segran, Fast Company

"Crouch knows the ins and outs of public relations like nobody else."

-SWAAY

UNKNOWN TO UNFORGETTABLE

*How to Stop Playing Small,
Land National Media Attention and
Position Yourself as a Power Player*

Ashley Crouch

ISBN-13: 978-1-64434-035-6

TABLE OF CONTENTS

Disclaimer 19

Welcome to Unknown to Unforgettable 21

Background 25

Why Media? 35

Raising Visibility 43

The Top 3 Reasons (You Think) You Should Not Invest in Media 51

Who Is This For? (And Who Is This Not For?) 57

One Myth and Some Other Concerns 63

Three New Principles 75

New Principle #1 79

The Archetype Approach: How to Create an Irresistibly Viral Angle 79

New Principle #2 91

Purposeful Planting: How to Land & Leverage Your Breakout Story 91

New Principle #3 105

Give Before You Get: Find & Connect with Media Influencers Without Spending Thousands 105

Epilogue 113

Why I Created Master the Media *Jumpstart* 121

WORKSHEETS 139

ABOUT THE AUTHOR 151

Dedication

This book is dedicated to the audacious men and women
who believe they have a mission, purpose, and big work to
do in the world… and to those who want to leverage the
enormous power of media to make an impact.

Just so you know, I put together a companion webinar that goes with this book, which you can check out right here (bit.ly/AshleyCompanionWebinar).

Disclaimer

What you are about to read is extremely powerful. The following methods are proven to land major national media attention, exponentially increase website traffic, and boost business growth.

However, this book does not guarantee that you will land media attention or grow your business. All the examples, principles, and strategies are proven and authentic, but ultimately your success at gaining visibility is all about you. The contents of this book are, quite literally, in your hands.

I have no legal advice or even formal training in the principles I am about to teach. Nonetheless, I have used these tactics to land 180 media features in eight months across seven countries for a no-name startup. I secured 65 media features in five weeks for a global conference that reached one hundred countries. In the meantime, I have taught two thousand everyday men and women just like you how to apply these principles and win. Want to be one of them?

Read on.

Welcome to Unknown to Unforgettable

This book is designed to offer no-fluff, results-driven guidelines on how to navigate the media landscape, bypass convention, and land big publicity without a big-ticket agency.

My method is designed for those people who want to make a difference, people who seek to "go big or go home" through a backdoor approach that is completely ethical and twice as fast.

The principles, strategies, and examples offered in this book are one hundred percent authentic and used by students and clients of mine in nine countries. These methods have allowed them to leverage media to position themselves as premier experts in their industry.

No matter where you are in business, you can land major national media attention. You can do it even if you have never been featured anywhere and are an introvert with no tech skills, who hates networking, flunked out of school, and prefers to sit at home in their pajamas eating Thai food.

My guess is you have a lot more going for you....

Maybe you are an employee with a side hustle, dreaming of going full time in business because you realize your 9 to 5 takes years of your life away making someone else's dreams come true.

You are underwhelmed with your boss, tired of the grind, and want to have more meaning and connection in your work. You want to position yourself as a premier personal brand, attract more clients and customers, and land your dream job or go out on your own with a new sense of freedom and purpose.

Perhaps you are an author, speaker, podcaster, or aspiring thought leader who wants to become an industry expert. You know you have a message to share with the world that will really help people, if only they knew you existed.

You would love to book more speaking opportunities—and get paid!—and perhaps even appear on TV. All you need is a proven plan.

Perhaps you have a non-profit and are bursting with stories you want to share about all your life-changing work, but you need clarity about how to structure those stories and you need maximum impact at an affordable price.

Perhaps you are a public relations (PR) professional trying to level up and keep your skills sharp in a changing world because you realize the principles that got you where you are won't take you where the world is headed.

Perhaps you are a business owner—this includes you, solopreneurs, coaches, and influencers—already working full time with clients and customers and ready to scale by jumping into this whole media world because you know it will somehow help you grow.

Or perhaps you are a hybrid of two or more of the above—yay for multi-passionate entrepreneurs! Whatever the reason you picked up this book, I will teach you actionable, practical strategies that you can begin to use immediately to level up your visibility and position yourself as a power player.

You are not alone anymore. Regardless of your "category," you are infused with a unifying thread that propels you forward day after day, urging you to leap out of bed and serve at a higher level.

You are a go-getter. You have a mission. You are ready to step into your great work in the world with renewed intention and make an impact. You are ready to take radical responsibility for your results and your lack thereof.

You have it in you, and you know it!

That's why you get jealous every time you see others making a difference in a big way. You know you can do it, too!

You know if someone would just peel back the curtain on the whole world of media, you could be just as successful. It is your time, but you want to do it right.

If any of these scenarios resonate with you, this is your book. I wrote it specifically for you.

Finally, I created a companion webinar that supports this book and that you can watch right here any time that suits you.

My treat: (bit.ly/AshleyCompanionWebinar).

Background

I remember it like it was yesterday. Five years ago this month, I was in France. It was my birthday and I was on a much-needed vacation after spending years working around the clock (including nights and weekends) at a new start-up fashion magazine, *Verily*.

To be honest, I was burned out. We had struggled for years, relocating to New York, going without paychecks, and living on hustle and caffeine as we tried to carve out a niche for ourselves to stand out in a saturated market filled with skeptics.

When the launch team of five women came together to start the company, we tried everything we could to get noticed. People thought our idea to launch a fashion magazine was crazy. Investors thought the market was oversaturated and that no one would care. Readers wondered how we were different. Family members reassured us we could "always move home." Yet we hustled. We dreamed. We cried. Every day, it felt like the future of our company hung in the balance and rested on my ill-equipped PR shoulders.

A few weeks prior to my birthday vacation, I walked into a meeting with Arianna Huffington's chief of staff and the senior style editor at *The Huffington Post*. I wore a brave face, but inside my stomach was in knots.

Will I say the right thing?

Will my boss be impressed?

Will we finally make a breakthrough?

Then I told the story of our start-up company and magazine. I explained how we wanted to help people and change the media landscape forever. In the meeting, I highlighted the steps we were taking to tackle that mission, and how people's lives were changing as a result.

They learned how we cast models off the street and put them in the pages of our fashion magazine. They saw how, in a culture of competition, we were on a mission to create a culture of affirmation.

When I saw their eyes light up, I thought, *We're in.*

Fast forward to my birthday. I woke up and checked my email.

The story about our company had just published in *The Huffington Post*!

It went absolutely *viral to seven countries*. The kind of viral that makes even *The Today Show* take notice and give you a call. (Yes, they called *us*.)

Happy birthday to me!!!

I was floating on cloud nine. Everything changed that day as we rode a tidal wave of media attention. Overall, we got 180 media features in eight months, including *Upworthy*, *The Queen Latifah Show*, *The Huffington Post*, *The Daily Telegraph* in Sydney, Australia, *Fox Business*, *Entrepreneur*, *CBS*, *SiriusXM Radio*, *Harper's Bazaar*, the *New York Post*, *New York Mag*.... Almost every major national platform was featuring our magazine.

We went from 30,000 views a month to 280,000 views a month in a matter of weeks. Later, the senior editor at *Huffington Post* told me, "Your pitch was one of the only cold pitches we have ever accepted."

I will teach you exactly how to achieve that result in just a minute.

After that huge growth spurt, the magazine closed four rounds of investor funding. We sold out in Barnes & Noble stores nationwide. We coordinated a national launch tour that convened bloggers, influencers, and celebrities. We hosted a smash hit launch party in New York City's swanky Soho district that turned our competitors green with envy. I directed photoshoots and even went to New York Fashion Week.

By sheer force of will, I found myself desk-side with editors at *The New York Times*, and in meetings with reporters for *E! News*, trying not to drool over their swoon-worthy, camera-ready wardrobe.

Eight years later, the magazine has over one million views per month.

Was everything sunshine, roses and red carpets? No. In fact, I moved to New York in pursuit of a dream only to spend an embarrassing number of days existing only off ramen and canned beans. Working from a "home office" often translated to being "homebound" because who had money for a $14 cocktail from the nearby dive bar? I projected judgment vibes from everyone who wrote me "We believe in you!" cards for graduation. There were plenty of days filled with crippling self-doubt, walks home from the office in ugly-cry tears, and paralyzing moments of fear as I wondered which action to take next. And coming from growing up in Arkansas on a farm with a hundred chickens, I experienced more than my fair share of culture shock (more on that later).

Simply put, when I was getting started, I had no formal media training, no background in PR, and no media connections whatsoever. I had no mentor and no help. Pitching the media felt like sending desperate messages out into a void—with my job and my future hanging in the balance.

One phone call to a friend of mine who happened to work in publicity at the time sounded something like this:

"It feels like I'm throwing spaghetti against the wall to see what sticks. Is this really how PR works?" I said in hushed tones.

To which my kind friend replied, "Yes, that's basically it."

So I kept on, gathering momentum from every successful story. Ten features, 20 features, 30 features, a new TV appearance, some influencer partnerships. Was it force of will? Was it luck? Was the world of PR just a lot of smoke and mirrors?

Then word started to get out about the successes, and I found myself in coffee shops with young graduates boasting shiny degrees in Public Relations and Mass Communications. They asked me, "What do I need to know to be successful in PR? How can I do what you do?"

I gave them the no-fluff, scrappy strategies I developed only to hear their response:

"I didn't learn any of that in school."

"Interesting," I replied, "because that is what works."

It was about the time *The Today Show* started contacting us and our social channels grew organically by over two-thousand percent across all platforms (propelled by the movement we created) that I realized just how powerful media can be. Over time, as the results continued to grow, I became a believer in this simple truth:

> "Media is the foundation of your business growth, but you have to do it in the right way."

Then I had an *ah-ha!* moment: if only more entrepreneurs could develop their story and leverage media attention, they would be able to accelerate and grow their businesses faster than ever before.

This is how I started codifying the methods that worked for me. This is how I started systematizing the techniques that got me massive results—while removing the errors and mistakes that caused me to do things the long and difficult way. Believe it or not, there are shocking mistakes that even celebrity publicists get wrong, which cost people like you thousands of dollars and hours of lost time.

This is why I developed this book: to give you the formulas and techniques that actually work so you can learn in mere hours what took me years to master. Until now, no one has outlined a comprehensive, step-by-step, proven system that allows everyday men and women to bypass convention and be heard.

Today, I am the founder of an award-winning PR agency, Appleseed Communications, that represents visionary entrepreneurs nationwide and teaches students in nine countries. Because I believe business is the fastest force for global change, we integrate social good right into the fabric of our work. For every client we serve, we offer a micro-loan to women entrepreneurs in resource-poor nations. To date, we have worked with women entrepreneurs in 21 nations, such as Cambodia, Malawi, Uganda, Mozambique, Kenya and more.

I have written for *The New York Times, Forbes.com, Fast Company, TIME.com, Business Insider, Refinery29, Mic., The Huffington Post, Thrive Global, Bust.com, The Everygirl*, and so many more.

In the last year alone, I taught two thousand people just like you—from bestselling authors to coaches, from former CEOs of multimillion-dollar companies to Forbes Under 30 Award-winners, from environmental advocates to fashion designers revolutionizing the industry, to nutrition experts, certified coaches, podcast hosts, thought leaders, and digital nomads.

These individuals have learned the principles that get results to become a Power Player in their industry. Almost daily I hear from students or clients who landed media attention in *Fast Company, O Magazine, Forbes, HelloGiggles, Shape,*

Thrive Global, and hundreds more. Call it my drug, but I get a rush when untold stories are heard and shared by the people who need them most.

The time has come for a book like this because the world is changing faster than ever. Globalization, technology, the growing popularity of digital business, and increased noise can leave you feeling like you are lost in a void, swimming in a saturated market, unsure of how to stand out from the crowd and thrive in a league of your own.

In the world we live in today, we need a better solution than simply throwing things against the wall and seeing what sticks.

Let's get started.

What You Will Learn in This Book:

- The Top 3 Reasons It Is Absolutely Vital to Land Media and Become a Power Player
- The 6 Reasons It Is Easier than Ever to Raise Visibility
- Top 3 Reasons (You Think) You Should Not Invest in Media
- Who This Is For and Who It Is Not For
- Top 4 Reasons Pitches Fail

- The 3 New Principles of PR Proven to Land National Media Attention
- The 4 Outlets You Should Prioritize to Grow Your Business

The contents of this book reveal techniques I've honed over almost a decade of scoring major press features for clients, including my exact strategy for choosing the right media platforms and the sneaky little tool I use to save thousands on media contact databases.

These three new principles are part of a proven method that allows you to bypass huge PR fees and get featured in top magazines and media outlets...all through a backdoor approach that is completely ethical and twice as fast.

Along the way, you will meet go-getter experts, just like you, to see exactly how they applied what I'm teaching you today to their business to skyrocket their success!

Ready to learn how you can create the gigantic megaphone you need to spread your message?

Let's Go!

Why Media?

We need to lay a foundation. You may have picked up this book wondering what PR is all about, or your friends may be telling you "you need PR." I will teach you content, but first it is important to understand context. So why is it SO crucial to get press for your business?

There are three main reasons to land visibility. All others are fluff. Two, you might already know, but the third one is going to take you by surprise:

1. **EXPOSURE.** You want to amplify your message to thousands or millions of potential readers, customers, or clients. Why? Because people can't *love* you and *buy* from you if they can't *find* you. The right press, done the right way, puts you in front of exactly the right people to change your business and your life. Many, many, many PR agencies and

strategies get this wrong.

In my recent Forbes article, I call out the industry for the mistakes they make and how it costs you big-time. Simply put, many publicists use a "spray-and-pray" method. It may result in stories, but such a method will not align with the target customer you are trying to reach and will ultimately be a waste of time and money.

I teach a completely different method, an empathy-first approach to think about your target customer, so every piece of publicity you receive will align with and attract them. More on that later, in Raising Visibility.

2. **CREDIBILITY.** In the world we live in today, media logos offer social proof. Media gives you credibility and legitimacy. It's that stamp of approval that your business is valued and vetted. You want to get that "As Seen In..." banner on your website because it builds a relationship of trust right away.

This is so important because it's so easy to start a business online, to set up shop and claim you are an expert. The founder of Airbnb Brian Chesky_(See page 137) said that an individual can become a business in 60 seconds, which is great news for you to diversify your income, build new revenue streams, or scale a company.

But the challenge is that, with so many people flooding the market claiming to be experts, it has become extremely difficult for your customers to know who they can trust. Lining up big media provides social proof that helps you rise above your competitors.

3. **POSITIONING.** This is the most overlooked benefit of visibility and why the art of visibility is the new critical life skill. All visibility is not the same. In my interview with Ali Brown_(See page 137), a growth strategist for seven-figure entrepreneurs, she says, "Positioning is what you stand for so other people instantly understand."

When you invest in appearing as an expert in major national media outlets, you are crafting a brand that stands the test of time. You need to know how to leverage media to position yourself in a category of one, to bypass the noise, the fluff, and become the obvious go-to choice for your clients and customers.

Why is this so important? The world has changed. I'm sure you feel it, too. We all know people who have lost their jobs suddenly with no second income or have chosen to launch a company in pursuit of financial freedom. You are not alone in this. Studies show that by the year 2020, between 40 and 50 percent of workers in the US will be freelance (See page 137). That's 60 million people flooding into the marketplace, competing for clients, projects, coverage, and customers in a crowded market.

Trying to stand out will be harder than ever. You have a window of time to position yourself, set yourself apart, and gain credibility from the media.

If you don't have exposure or visibility, you are probably relying on word-of-mouth referral leads or expensive paid traffic that doesn't always give the results you want.

You may be experiencing a feast-or-famine cycle in your business that makes you wonder if you can pay your bills next month. You cannot plan for your future, much less your next vacation. You could be five or even 10 years into your business and people still don't know who you are.

Not exactly what you dreamed about, right?

Landing your breakout media story is the FOUNDATION of your business growth, but you have to do it the right way. That foundation is the exposure, credibility, and positioning you build upon. That up-front investment in landing media attention will pay off for years to come.

The success of your business relies on the right visibility. It does not matter if you have a juicier origin story than Wonder Woman and a product more revolutionary than the smartphone. If no one's talking about it, you won't have a business.

When you focus on getting the right visibility, everything in your business shifts. Here are four side-effects you might enjoy:

1. **Clients & Customers Fall from the Sky.** Not literally, but when people read about you in *Forbes* or *O Magazine*, you don't have to work so hard to find customers. Leads drop into your lap without you having to desperately chase them.

2. **People Are Willing to Pay You More $$$.** Who would you pay big money to work with? the life coach who friended you on Facebook and bullied you into a free consultation or the life coach you saw featured on *mindbodygreen* and *Inc.* last month? Read on to find out how my student 5x'ed her prices and no one batted an eye.

3. You Sell Without Selling. Hate doing sales calls? Feel like you're practically begging for the sale and offering way too many discounts and fringe benefits?

Media attention = pre-sold customers who do not need to hear your long-winded sales pitch. They are ready to buy...like, yesterday.

4. Your Business Becomes Scalable. Transitioning from one-to-one client work to group programs? Want to turn your one-man shop into a full-scale agency? Want to drive more traffic and leads to your website, grow your email list, or experience the sweet feeling of people sliding into your DMs with invitations for you to speak on stage, or offers to work together? All it takes is the right visibility.

If you want your business to be viable, it's time to start getting visible. There is just a tiny window of time between now and 2020 to really take your visibility seriously so you don't get left behind.

You came to the right place.

Now that we are on the same page about why it is so important to land the right visibility, read on for the rebel's guide to landing media like a royal so you can position yourself as a power player and make your mark.

*Full disclosure: It may not be for everyone and that is ok. A couple times later on, my straight talk, direct points, and ruckus-making challenges might make you feel uncomfortable. Few things strike fear like stepping forward to own your power, become the face of a mission, and get noticed.

Remember: *you are so brave. You are so bold.*

Do you want me to offer fancy fluff or straight talk that gets you the result you want? I prefer the latter. Please know I say all things with (tough) love because I have been where you are, pursuing a dream, seeking a goal and I found a proven way to achieve it. You can, too, if you stick with me.

Let's link arms and get this done.

Raising Visibility

Ready to get started but feeling overwhelmed? Here is some good news:

It is easier than ever for the average person to get media attention.

You can get booked faster, in bigger outlets, without a PR agency—all with no press release, no prior knowledge, and no tech skills whatsoever. In fact, this could be your advantage.

(Cue the dancing.)

I'm not just saying that. I've personally witnessed a first-time author with no prior media experience start getting attention within 24 hours using the techniques I can teach you. Since then, she has written for *Thrive Global* and secured many more media features for her message.

Another startup female founder took the lessons in this book to place herself front and center on the list of Oprah's Favorite Things...within weeks.

These stories are just two of countless cases. And you could be next. The landscape of public relations has dramatically shifted in the past ten years, allowing individuals to hold more power than ever before. Here are six changes you need to know about:

1. The rise of social media has democratized how stories are heard, shared, and picked up by the more "traditional" media outlets. It has given the average person access to top journalists to pitch story ideas and share those stories with a global audience. Some stories even go viral in a matter of hours with global hashtags such as the #MeToo movement.

2. Media outlets have become increasingly fragmented, specialized, and niche, which allows for higher concentrations of specific audiences that could help generate greater return on investment (ROI). This means you get in front of exactly the right audience, which could mean more conversions (and money!) for you. On the other hand, it also allows groups of

people to silo themselves off from one another, creating cultural blind spots. Political groups are often caught off guard by the success of various candidates because they truly "never saw it coming."

3. Stories are pitched and shared in less formalized ways than ever (encouragement to share on social, take action, sign a petition). Press releases are much less effective, and many stories get pitched through text message, social media DMs, or growth-hacking techniques baked into the product or company itself. I teach people how to share their stories in pitch letters for maximum impact. It is easier than ever, if one has the skills.

4. Companies can generate their own "media" through video and content creation, then cross-publish it on large, national, and global outlets, such as *The Huffington Post* or *Thrive Global*. Or articles can go "viral" on platforms like LinkedIn and lead to television opportunities for the thought leader.

5. Staff writers within media outlets are being let go at accelerated rates, creating a vast pool of high-quality freelance journalists that write for many outlets. If a person knows how to find them and build relationships, it can increase their chances of being

featured on national platforms because there are many outlets to which one journalist could send the story.

6. PR was once often considered a luxury available only to large companies with big budgets. Today, I consider it the new critical life skill that all individuals can and should learn. You hold in your hands a blueprint to get there.

It has never been easier to generate high-quality media attention, yet PR is often the missing piece that holds companies back from growth. You could be spending thousands of dollars for an on-demand (CMO) and Facebook (FB) ad spend that rivals your mortgage, but if you don't have media exposure, credibility, and positioning, you are leaving thousands of dollars on the table.

I get it. The industry seems confusing. You do not know who to trust or how to track ROI. Additionally, many publicists and PR trainers teach an upside-down approach that takes too much time, results in less impactful media appearances, and does not drive credibility or growth. Here's why:

1. **Spray and pray method.** Effective PR tells the story the brand wants to tell to the audience that most wants to hear it. Many publicists, however, operate under the spray and pray method. For example, they

pitch a combination of outlets that may not align with the target customer you want to reach. You may get a press "win," but it does not drive traffic or improve the bottom line because there was no alignment with the target customer. Landing a media story may bolster the credibility of the publicist, but it could do little to advance your business. Instead, start with empathy and match the outlet to the target for maximum results.

2. **Lack of alignment.** Did you land a national feature that did not move the needle in your business? The answer could be lack of alignment between platform and story angle. Many publicists leave the story angle to chance. They rely on pre-existing relationships and allow the reporter to find the angle. Instead, discover the story from within the brand's essence, craft the story to attract the target customer, and identify the reporter best fit to tell it. This ensures there is a match between the brand's story and the target customer you are trying to reach.

3. **Starting small.** Many PR trainers advise you to start at the bottom, approach local, small podcasts and blogs, and work your way up to national platforms. While this may give you practice refining your message, the method is problematic for multiple

reasons. First, early-stage entrepreneurs are limited in both time and resources. Instead of pitching small outlets that take the same amount of time and energy for a press feature that will not drive traffic, you should prepare to land your breakout major media story first in a larger or national platform. This will drive more traffic. Second, when you land a breakout story in a larger platform, smaller outlets will get in line to feature you. The result is more features with less time and effort, offering more credibility, exposure, and positioning.

Are you ready to be on the front page? Here are a couple of things to keep in mind:

You don't have to be perfect to get started. In fact, I tell my students "practice makes progress and progress is the point." Just follow along with the methods in this book. All you have to do is say yes to show up and try out these techniques. That's it. You just have to show up and try. Deal?

In the following chapters, I will outline the principles and strategies you can use to get results. But I am not promising it will be a cake walk. My system is not for people who are comfortable playing small. So if that is you, please close the book right now. My goal is to challenge you to step forward and face what obstacles may hold you back from getting the results you desire, so you can burst onto the national stage and blast through those roadblocks on your way to success. I will offer you the time-tested tools I use as well as guidelines to help you bypass the massive mistakes that even celebrity publicists make. (The media will thank you!)

Once you know how to do this correctly, getting that national and international press will amplify your reach, explode your viewership, give you a massive brand-awareness boost, and help you build relationships with people and outlets that can't wait to support your vision.

Stick with me, you're in good hands.

TAKE ACTION

Remember your why.
If media could help you achieve
Anything in the next six months,
what would that be?

_____

_____

_____

_____

_____

_____

_____

_____

_____

_____

_____

_____

_____

_____

_____

_____

_____

_____

_____

The Top 3 Reasons (You Think) You Should Not Invest in Media

You don't need to wait months or years for huge press. You just need to know how to use my step-by step-system to gaining massive exposure, fast. However, there are three things getting in your way.

We need to call out the elephant in the room about what is holding you back. (Don't worry, this is a safe space to take an honest look at the excuses getting in your way, so you can move forward.) In my work with almost two thousand people in the last year, I found these to be the top three obstacles:

No urgency: The first obstacle is that you're actually doing pretty well. You're comfortable. You are making a living. You don't NEED more money. You have a decent-paying job or business and there is no critical drive to move into new territory. You have hit your "comfort plateau."

You know you hit a comfort plateau when your mind invents excuses to justify inaction. Thoughts will flood your mind, such as:

Who am I to get the limelight?

Am I sure I am really ready?

Maybe I don't really need this.

Maybe my product is not worth getting a feature in a national outlet...or any outlet.

Beware of this phase. Once you hit that plateau, you're not just standing still. You're backsliding...and your competitors are rapidly catching up.

To overcome this obstacle, remember: *you are the fuel for your business.*

Your business rises to the level that you do. If there is no momentum inside your business, it is because there is no momentum inside of you.

Think of your business as a mirror and your life will change. Besides, every movement needs a figurehead. So you owe it to yourself and everyone you serve to get visible.

> **Think of your business as a mirror and your life will change.**

No focus: You might think there are other priorities—make the product better, build a better website, finish your headshots, land a client that pays the bills. After training two thousand people in the last year, I have seen over and over how so many entrepreneurs chase money or focus on the fluff. In this phase, you are in danger of becoming a "perfectionist producer"—making sure the product is *perfect* before getting exposure for it.

To overcome this obstacle, remember that if you land the right exposure, those paying clients will take you more seriously, and you will be able to charge premium rates and sell faster. Then you will have more capital and credibility to invest in the branding, website, headshots, and product improvement.

No system: Time is short. You don't know who to trust or how to measure ROI. This entire PR world feels mysterious and not worth your time. You need a proven system. You have a to-do list a mile long, but you are practical, and you want to invest in activities that generate immediate ROI.

Meanwhile, you get jealous of all the "overnight successes" crowding up your newsfeed. Let's do a little thought experiment:

Ever notice how some people seem to come out of nowhere? Suddenly, they have all the right connections. They are featured in *Forbes, Fast Company, O Magazine, Entrepreneur, mindbodygreen, The Knot, Glamour, Refinery29,* and *Brit & Co.*

They have prestigious partnerships and speaking opportunities. They write for all the top outlets. They have everything they need to help their company grow faster than yours.

Meanwhile, you work around the clock, feeling stuck, underpaid, overworked…and secretly jealous. You keep grinding away trying to build a great product that should be blatantly obvious people should buy, but your list of prospects is more barren than the Sahara desert. It seems so easy for them, like your peers have the Midas touch.

The truth is, there is a system and a formula that they know. But good news. You can learn it, too!

To overcome this obstacle, remember: *raising visibility is possible for everyone. Really. Let that sink in.*

Full disclosure: in the following chapters I am going to turn the traditional PR industry on its head. This will be unlike other PR training you have heard or learned before. I will not teach you how to play small. My system works for people ready to step forward into their role as a power player and make a real difference in the world. If that is you, keep going.

TAKE ACTION:

**Of these three, which is your biggest obstacle?
Name it and claim it below.**

Once you know the culprit, you can move forward.

In the meantime, here are 3 affirmations to reset
your mind for visibility success:

1. I have a message I was born to contribute.
2. I don't just have a message; I am the message.
3. My story offers value to everyone I meet.

_____
_____
_____
_____
_____
_____
_____
_____
_____
_____
_____
_____

Who Is This For?
(And Who Is This Not For?)

As I explained before, the media today is completely democratized. Never before in the history of the planet has the ability to land a breakout media story been more accessible than it is today. But you don't need to stage a "wardrobe malfunction" to get featured on *Global*. It's not about knowing the right people, or kowtowing to some guy in a suit.

The age of the Internet has proven one thing: You can be your own publicist.

You can go from hanging out in the shadows, feeling unknown, to being unforgettable.

Imagine getting featured on the front page of *The New York Times* business section with ZERO previous media coverage.

You have that ability, right now...today. All you need is a blueprint and this book will give it to you.

If you like what you read here and want to go deeper, there is an opportunity to work together with one of our white glove packages later on.

That said, let's get clear on a few things. My system is not for everyone.

This book is for you if...

➢ **You have a tantalizing "origin story" you just know the media would eat up.**

Why did you get into the business you're in? I'm betting it's not the career your parents dreamed of for you, and probably not what you studied in college either. Whatever it is, we'll polish that story up until it's so shiny all the major media outlets will be clamoring to publish it.

➢ **Your business solves a real problem.**

I'm not saying you should have the cure for cancer. But you do need to offer a valid solution to something your ideal customer is suffering from. We're here to hone that.

➢ **You want to make a bigger contribution in your business.**

Your business is about more than money—though you're happy to collect the dosh AND make an impact with your epic product or service. What you offer could quite literally mean life or death—or at least a huge improvement in quality—for so many. You owe it to those people to help them find you.

➢ **You have a proven business model. You just need more people to know about it.**

You are getting ready to launch in the next few months, or already have happy clients and customers who are saying great things about you, but you'd like to have a whole lot more.

You want to bypass the slow and steady method to supercharge your results.

> **You're a natural action taker; all you need is the action plan.**

If you're tired of doing the wrong activities, join the club. This book will leverage your natural inclination to get sh*t done and show you the path to *superfast* results.

This book is NOT for you if:

> **You think it's egotistical to try to get media attention.**

If you're going to land major media attention, you need to really want it—with zero judgment on yourself. Landing national media attention requires an attitude of service and generosity, which I will outline later.

> **You have no idea what you want to be known for or who your target audience is.**

This book is for people who are clear on their mission and who they want to serve.

> **You prefer to have someone else do PR for you, and you have the budget for it.**

Self-explanatory, right? May I suggest a cheaper route? Read this book and hand if off to your assistant or PR team. It's better than dropping $70,000, plus now you've got an in-house team getting you coverage 365 days a year.

> **You flip-flop between ideas and struggle to commit to one thing.**

I won't ask you to give up your multiple passion projects, but I DO need you to focus on one business at a time. When it comes to landing media attention, the fortune is in the follow-through. So you need to be committed.

> **You're looking for a magic bullet and not prepared to show up and do the work.**

If you don't get that bringing the PR magic is literally ALL ABOUT YOU, then this isn't for you. On the other hand, if you are prepared to do the work, I (literally) guarantee you'll get media attention.

> **You want more PR clients.**

Want to hack my system, update your LinkedIn headline to "PR Expert" and get a job or build an agency of your own? All the love for publicists who want to level up their skills and continue learning. I heart you and so glad you are here. This book will help you, I promise. This book is not intended to be a certification manual to give you credibility as an expert, however. Many of my students *have* successfully used the lessons in this book to get their clients columns in *Harvard Business Review, Forbes, Thrive Global,* and more. This book makes no claims on how you will perform as a publicist for any third parties. I'm here to help you do PR for yourself. Hope that's clear.

One Myth and Some Other Concerns

"The feature is making it rain up in here!"

That is what my client Elana wrote me when her product landed on the front of a story in the *International Business Times.*

Elana had a good nine-to-five job, but one trip to Kenya opened her eyes to the poverty and inequality that still exists in the world, and she became determined to fix it. She left her steady paycheck to build a business that gives back to widowed women in Kenya with her company.

She had some small wins, but she wanted to go bigger. We did a holiday campaign around her jewelry line to help her hit her goals.

Myth: Media Will Guarantee Sales

Because you're all wondering, publicity can never guarantee sales (and I am the first person who will say that!) nor should you want it to. That said, I have heard over and over again how one feature brought about five thousand orders, or $100,000 in business, and along with it, credibility and legitimacy. In the case of Elana, however, her media feature in a national outlet did convert to explosive revenue.

Here are some common questions you may be asking:

How do I measure ROI?

In case it bears repeating, PR is the foundation of your business growth, but you have to do it in the right way. This means you need to land media attention at the outset of your growth strategy and have a long-term vision in mind. Your personal and professional brand will become a platform that helps your sales process run more smoothly, often generating prospects, traffic, and list growth for years to come.

So don't expect media or PR to result in click-to-convert revenue. That is for your ad dollars. Media positions you as a power player and opens doors to speaking opportunities, partnership and sponsorship opportunities, social media growth, and volumes of brand credibility and loyalty. That web of relationships, partnerships, and featured stories will be tools you build upon. This is why if you are only investing in FB ads, driving traffic to a product or web page with no media credibility or positioning, you are leaving thousands of dollars on the table.

Customers will buy from you faster if you are vetted and positioned correctly. Remember, you are investing in your brand—both personal and professional—and it will pay off in dividends down the road for the reasons mentioned above. Do it right and invest in media attention first, then run advertising campaigns to a platform that is ready to convince and convert.

I am already so busy.
How much time do I have to invest to see results?

I'd love for ten percent of your resources to be focused on visibility, but I get that you might have to work up to that. (Once you see the results, you'll be HAPPY to do it!) In the meantime, you only need to invest one hour a week in amplifying your business.

Yeah, one hour, that's it! Less time than it takes you to drink that lux champagne (treat yourself!). You can subtract it from all those useless hours you spend scrolling your social media feeds.

I'm a mob boss/used car saleswoman/etc. I run a totally unique business. Will this book apply?

Absolutely. You do NOT need to be in a specific type of business to apply what I teach. Online or brick-and-mortar, I've used these techniques for all types of businesses in my agency, Appleseed Communications. They work.

Yeah, but what if it doesn't work for me?

Listen, when I first developed this system for myself, I had zero media contacts. None. I built all the amazing relationships I have with *Forbes, Inc., Fast Company, Refinery29, Hello Giggles, Brit & Co, The New York Times, Thrive Global, Entrepreneur*, and more using this exact system. It works.

How long does it take to see results?

Previous clients and students have landed major media like *Thrive Global, Hello Giggles, Shape, mindbodygreen, American Express Open Forum, Buzzfeed,* and *Fast Company* in as little as 24 hours or just a few weeks.

How do I know if I'm ready?

Do you have a business that could benefit from being seen and heard by more people around the world? Are you committed to putting in the money and time to support that vision? Then it's simple. You're ready.

Will this work if I don't live in the US?

Yes! I've taught business owners from all over the world, and the principles and system taught in this book work around the globe.

Can I just send a press release?

Three words: Don't do it. Attachments are rarely - if ever - opened or read. PR newswires cost volumes of money. The resulting story lacks intrigue, reach, and alignment with your target customer. To this day, people write press releases and get featured in ABC, Fox, MSNBC. It looks shiny and glittery on the outside and they consider it a win. But they confide in me that no one saw the story and it drove no traffic to their cause. This is because press release features are published on parts of the website no one ever reads. And remember, there is no alignment with the target customer (as mentioned earlier). It is a waste of time. Press releases are announcements. What you want to create is a story. I'll teach you how in a minute.

Can I just invest in FB ads?

FB ads are great, but if you pour volumes of money into a funnel to drive traffic to a website with no social proof, no credibility, no positioning...you are leaving thousands of dollars on the table. Who would you rather hire? The business coach seen in *Forbes, Fast Company*, and *Inc*, or the one with a testimony from their mother? The choice is obvious. Master your messaging and your media first, then accelerate the growth with Facebook ads.

What if I just want to go to networking events?

There is power in proximity to the right people. It is important to build a great network but consider this... you could attend networking events where everyone is at the same level of business as you are, struggling to make money by selling to each other and squeezing juice from a turnip. These events are fun, and I've been to more than my fair share of networking events in sassy locations from LA to NYC, Boston to Israel.

Between you and me, when I got serious, I made a spreadsheet and tracked where every single lead and new client came from in my business. After a year, the results were eye-opening. That exclusive "inner circle" summit for the exclusive Who's Who of the world that I shelled out thousands to attend? No new clients. That glittery conference with all the A-list celebrities speaking? No new clients. While getting clients is just one factor of success, if you have precious little time and need to keep the lights on in your business, you need cash and clients and they are attracted to perfectly positioned power players.

Straight talk: Business needs the funding fuel to keep running. Instead of feeling cool by attending more events (and maybe you could still attend some events if that is your thing, for coaching, masterminds, or other venues), I invite you to consider another option. You could leverage your time by sitting in the comfort of your home feeling fabulous while the influential media power players refer you to their readers in a media story and tag you repeatedly on Twitter, Facebook, and Instagram, sending referrals sliding into your dms on the regular. Invest in your brand that pays you big bucks. And who knows? Maybe you host your own fantasy event in exotic locations and people pay YOU to attend. Wouldn't that be a fun shift? Just sayin'…

What if I don't have a story?

As I mentioned, if I can do this, you can do it. I grew up at the end of a dirt road in Arkansas on a farm with one hundred chickens. I wore denim, ankle-length skirts, was barefoot more often than not, and rode horses on the weekends. I always felt a little different. Yet despite how I looked or where I grew up, I always had a one big dream: I wanted more.

I never thought in a million years that I would be the first woman to graduate from college on both sides of my family.

I never thought I would move to New York City and launch *Verily*, the first "no-Photoshop" fashion magazine.

I never thought I would contribute to *Forbes*.

I never thought I would run a global business that impacts the lives of women entrepreneurs in 21 resource-poor nations.

Remember: *We all start somewhere!*

I started somewhere at the end of a dirt road in Arkansas.

You started somewhere, too.

I used to be shy about sharing my story, so I told other people's stories for a living. But then I realized: **The most important story we will ever tell is the one we tell ourselves**...about what is possible.

What is the story you tell yourself? *Why* do you want to play a bigger game? Get this dialed in and it will fuel you to the highest heights.

You have a message you were born to contribute. You have a way to make the world a better place. You can hide it or share it to propel yourself (and others) forward. But if you choose to share it, you have to do it in the right way! Many of us live by the story that leadership is for other people. Yet when we watch others get more attention, book more clients, make a bigger difference, a voice inside us whispers: *that should be me.*

That restlessness is your permission.

Are you ready to finally set aside the excuses and step forward?

If you've already gotten press features, then I have some great tips to help you position yourself in a way that gets you even more features, and faster.

And if you've never been featured before, you are in the perfect position to learn how to kick start your publicity so you can quickly and efficiently pave the way for a powerful launch, keep the momentum of your business growing, or continue to scale.

You don't just have a message. You are the message.

Let's dive in.

TAKE ACTION

Are you ready to move forward?
Yes or no?

_____

_____

_____

_____

_____

_____

_____

_____

_____

_____

_____

_____

_____

_____

_____

_____

_____

_____

_____

_____

Three New Principles

Businesses need three basic things to be successful: (1) a great product, (2) funding in the form of paying clients, customers, or investors, and (3) a powerful story. Which comes first? As it turns out, it's your story. Not every business requires venture capital to be successful. But a company with funding but no story can fall flat.

Conversely, a company with a great story and no funding may be able to secure by proving interest in the business model with high end media features. With a story and by using these tried-and-true strategies, you can get big media attention, even if you're "no one" in the eyes of the media right now.

What I teach is radically different from most publicists and PR trainers. Lots of people in PR teach you to start at the bottom and slowly work up. Conventional wisdom says to pitch blogs and small podcasts to start, then maybe local press, and approach the national outlets last.

Don't do it. Don't fall for conventional wisdom to start small. It is a waste of time. (The only exception to this is if you want to go on TODAY or Good Morning America or top National TV shows. They will often want a sizzle reel to prove you won't crumble on camera, so starting with local TV is helpful. Other than that - for all the podcasts, digital platforms, top brands - go as big as you dare.)

But I say, if you have finite time, then why waste it pitching tiny outlets that will have ZERO effect on your traffic and credibility?

If you land national platforms, then the credibility you gain opens more doors and all the other media outlets will come to you. It's the fastest way to grow your business using publicity, giving you a massive megaphone to amplify your message and reach.

And landing major media exposure can be a game changer for your business. Imagine Oprah recommending one of your products or your book. What do you think that would do for your business? Having national press feature you or your business is POWERFUL!

And with paid traffic costs rising, with television commercials out of reach for many business owners, and with more and more saturation in the online market, media exposure is becoming more valuable than ever before.

But of course, you first have to know how to land those major media features, especially when you don't have previous exposure. Good news. I codified my method into a proven training program that gives you on-demand access to the top techniques that work today, so you can bypass all the frustration and get right to the results. But for now, here is my high level step-by-step system for optimal impact, developed after years of hacking the system for maximum results.

You see, when I was getting started doing PR, I came into the industry a naive newbie. No one taught me to write a press release (again, don't do it, it will not work), how to pitch, or how to land a story... much less one that goes viral. But I had fire in my soul and a keen desire to get results; otherwise I would get fired and have to go home to live with my parents in the basement. Love mom and dad, but that felt incomprehensible.

So I took action and figured out why the world of media seems so off limits and what you can do about it.

The truth is, it might seem like the media is an exclusive club where only a few people ever get featured, but that is not the case. Hundreds, THOUSANDS, of media segments, profiles, and stories are created every single day. You are doing the media a favor by contacting them, because they are always looking for good stories!

The old ways of doing PR do not work as well anymore. There are easier, faster, more affordable routes to the top to help you bypass the clog because the world has changed... and the odds are ever more in your favor.

But PR agencies continue to charge high ticket prices to use outdated methodologies leaving you with underwhelming results, empty wallets, and a whole lot of frustration.

So I am going to give you a path forward.

The key to getting that media attention is by following the three new principles:

- *Principle #1 – The Archetype Approach*
- *Principle #2 – Principled Planting*
- *Principle #3 – Give Before You Get*

Read on to learn how each of these principles work.

New Principle #1

The Archetype Approach:
How to Create an Irresistibly Viral Angle

Writers contributing to big national media platforms are always looking for stories. As such, some of them get pitched thousands of times a day. But they rarely see a great story in their inbox. One day, an editor friend at *Forbes* told me, "Ashley, I get three thousand pitch emails per *week*!" Journalists are swamped, deadlines are tight, and if you pitch without the right method, it will be a small miracle if you hear back.

That's because people simply don't know how to structure their unique stories in a way that engages an audience and makes people on the other side of a pitch sit up and take notice. (No, it has nothing to do with press releases.) Since I started writing for *Forbes*, I get pitched a lot, and it is shocking to me how many people get it wrong—even celebrity publicists pitch me and make these same mistakes over and over. I am going to teach you how to avoid making those mistakes so you can get more press faster!

Here's why most pitch emails never get opened, and even fewer get read word-by-word.

REASON 1: YOU NEVER ACTUALLY HIT "SEND"

You've got 101 excuses for not sending that pitch email. You're not sure what to say. You don't know who to send it to. You wonder if your story is compelling enough.

Once you figure out your angle and your audience, you have no excuse for not sending that email. So do it and soon you'll be firing off pitch emails four to five times a week without breaking a sweat!

REASON 2: YOU DON'T KNOW WHO TO PITCH

It's so discouraging to work hard on a pitch only to hear crickets, but 99.9% of pitches simply land in the wrong inbox. When you get clear on who's looking for a story like yours, and you know where to find up-to-date contact information, you're a hundred times more likely to get from "pitched" to "published."

REASON 3: YOU MAKE IT TOO HARD TO SAY "YES"

Successful pitches make it easy as a can of spaghetti for a journalist to say, "Yes!" They're carefully outlined with three to five story angles and possible headlines. They're so well constructed that it would be more work for an editor NOT to publish them.

REASON 4: YOUR HEADLINE IS A ROTTEN EGG

Your email subject line is the number one thing that gets you noticed. No stunning opener = no opening at all. Top contributors to *Forbes* and *Inc.* get thousands of pitches a day. Unless your subject line stands out like a pink Cadillac at a football game, you aren't getting past the 30-yard line.

That's where my story archetypes come into play. I developed them while writing hundreds of headlines for *Psychology Today*. For a year, I wrote headlines for 35 articles a week to an audience of seven million. That's a lot of headlines. In the process, I noticed patterns in the stories that really engaged people, and I distilled that info into archetypes that anyone can use.

In my program with high levels of support, white glove service, and curated media opportunities, I deliver 13 story archetypes to you on a silver platter. In the interest of time, I will share three with you now. These are archetypes that you can use right away. Take a look at just how powerful they really are.

THE UNEXPECTED TWIST:

The first story I want to tell you is my own. It's how I got international press for our startup fashion magazine, *Verily*, and it involved finding the PERFECT angle for what the magazine did and why that mattered.

When I was invited to be on the founding team for *Verily*, I moved to New York City, and soon our tiny team of five women were working around the clock, nights and weekends, trying to get the word out about this new start-up. It didn't take long before investors and readers began asking us, "Why are you launching another print fashion magazine? Isn't it an already saturated market?"

When you're just starting in a new venture, this is not a question you want to hear. Like many service providers, thought leaders, authors, and coaches who are just finding their feet, we felt we were one of many, and we were working 24/7 trying to differentiate, trying to attract the right clients, but at first, we felt like we were just spinning our wheels. So I approached the team and explained how we need language to talk about this magazine. We are not getting any traction because no one understands what really makes us unique. **We need an angle that people will remember.**

And so I branded *Verily* as the first no-Photoshop magazine in existence. I felt that somewhere out there were other women who also wanted to feel like they were enough and who would like to be celebrated for the best of who they already were, without alteration or manipulation.

We went from 30,000 views a month to 280,000 views a month in a matter of weeks. All of that coverage started with that single archetype: **The Unexpected Twist**. Most people send pitches like announcements. "Hello, we just started this new thing and it's really cool." If I had pitched Verily like an announcement, I would have heard crickets; there are many new ventures started every day. Instead, I pitched a story about five unlikely women challenging the culture of competition by creating the world's first no-Photoshop fashion magazine. See how that adds an unexpected twist? (I can teach you how to find your angle, so you go from unknown to unforgettable, too.)

By creating the concept of the world's first no-Photoshop fashion magazine, I created a story that people wanted to write about in major national platforms, and soon everyone else came clamoring for more. Story is one of the most powerful tools you can use to get your pitches picked up. After all, that's what writers write. And if you give them the story idea, you make it so much easier for them to write about YOU!

As it turned out, our unexpected twist led to us getting a huge breakout story in the *New York Post*.

LOW-TO-HIGH:

Another example of a great archetype? My clients Heather and Nora, founders of ImageThink. ImageThink is a company of artists who draw with markers. They visit offices like Google and draw the notes of executive strategy meetings. Such a cool idea, right?

But when the founders, Heather and Nora, started out, the initial idea for their business was merely drawn on the back of a spare napkin. They were waiting tables to pay the rent, trying to support their art. They didn't have a compelling angle. They had no archetype around their story.

These days that napkin is framed in the office of their multimillion-dollar company.

When ImageThink came to me to amplify their business in the hopes of getting more speaking gigs, I decided to use my **Low-to-High** story archetype. It's a rags-to-riches tale.

Here's how it looked in one headline:

> **"Entrepreneur Duo Transform An Idea From the Back of a Napkin"**

They started out drawing on napkins, and now they run a hugely successful business. Who doesn't want to hear that story, right?

Think about it: "Entrepreneur Duo Build a Multimillion-Dollar Business." That's expected.

Nothing very exciting, right?

Add: "from an Idea on the Back of a Napkin," and suddenly you're intrigued. Whoa. A multimillion-dollar business from a napkin? Tell me more!

The coverage we secured for them by pitching these kinds of stories resulted in many speaking gigs, including a keynote speaking opportunity in front of 11,000 people at the Massachusetts Conference for Women, the largest women's conference in the country. It was a sea of people. Can you imagine how much you could grow your business presenting as an expert in front of such an audience?

PRACTICAL AND ACTIONABLE:

I say, everyone is an expert at something. Whether you are a stay-at-home mom of five in the midwest, or a CEO who holds a P.h.D. and runs a team of 100 in some bustling city. You are an expert

As an expert, you have something to teach. So what can you teach and how will it help you raise national media attention? This is where my signature system is so valuable.

Remember how earlier we talked about how most PR agencies cost you thousands of dollars and lost time and money because they operate by a "spray and pray" principle? I am different.

I teach an "empathy first" approach and here's how you use it. First, consider who your target customer is. When you pitch the media, create a headline that will attract your target customer to click on it by teaching the solution to the problem that they have.

Let's see how this works in practice. My client *Julia Pimsleur, author of Million Dollar Women: The Essential Guide for Female Entrepreneurs Who Want to Go Big,* wanted to land national media when her book came out in print. As an author, she has wisdom on how women entrepreneurs can streamline and scale their businesses to 7 figures. So, we created a Practical and Actionable story angle that got her into CNBC Make It with a full profile.

Here's how it looks when published:

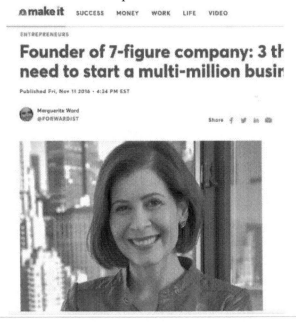

make it   SUCCESS   MONEY   WORK   LIFE   VIDEO

ENTREPRENEURS

Founder of 7-figure company: 3 th need to start a multi-million busir

Published Fri, Nov 11 2016 · 4:34 PM EST

Marguerite Ward
@FORWARDIST

Share f 𝕏 in

Image Think also had Practical and Actionable story archetypes in their business and this got them into MSNBC. Notice the headline below.

(*You can have multiple story archetypes in one business). Next time you want to pitch with this archetype, start here:

7 Strategies To Streamline...
3 Little-Known Hacks To...
5 Unexpected Techniques That...

And remember, always solve the problem your target customer has.

The next time you sit down to write a pitch, see if you can add an Unexpected Twist or the Low-to-High, or Practical and Actionable Archetype to your pitch to get people excited about writing and sharing your story. I've taught these and other archetypes to two thousand students who, just like you, had no idea what the media wants to write about. If they can do it, so can you.

Now you have your angle in hand. But how do you get major coverage from the outlets you're craving attention from? How do you get their attention? Read on for the next step in this proven system.

New Principle #2

Purposeful Planting:
How to Land & Leverage Your Breakout Story

So many people don't believe they can land major media exposure since they've never been featured. You may think that, too.

But I'm going to show you exactly how I did just that for *Verily* magazine back when I had no existing media contacts—and I'm going to tell you exactly what types of press outlets to focus on, depending on YOUR industry and business.

I'm guessing you've seen dandelions before. They're those puffy little balls you used to pick up as a child and blow on so you could watch all their little seeds float away on the breeze.

Now, what you might not know about dandelions is that each of those tiny puffs has more than 150 seeds on it. A lot of them get eaten by birds, a lot of them get buried, but most of them don't land where they can successfully grow and make more dandelions.

(Wondering why I'm talking about weeds? Bear with me; I promise I'm going somewhere.)

Now, for a long time, the traditional PR approach has been to take a huge breath and just blow on a dandelion, trying to scatter seeds as far and as wide as you can. This is called the "spray and pray" approach, meaning you just scattershot your leads as widely as you can and hope something works out.

The idea is that at least one of those dandelion seeds—at least one of your many press releases or phone calls or feature requests, etc.—will take root and result in big press for you and your business. And then before you know it, that one seed will grow exponentially and soon there will be a TON of dandelions, a.k.a. press coverage. But it takes so much effort and so many dandelion puffs and so many wasted seeds to do it that way.

Now, don't get me wrong. It is important to send out multiple pitches. But what if you knew exactly where to plant them, and you could blow your PR "seeds" in THAT right direction so more of them could land and take root?

If your PR strategy is a dandelion puff, and your pitches are the seeds on that puff, then knowing where to plant them means purposely picking the press outlets *that are the right fit for you.*

That's the first step. You need to map out your media plan. Where are you going to blow your seeds?

Many people never pitch themselves at all because they don't know how to create a plan. So consider your goals. Remember, you want exposure, credibility, and positioning.

To achieve this, prioritize top-tier media platforms that are aligned with your target customer.

You need to take an "empathy-first" approach. Purposefully planting your pitch involves alignment. You already have your story archetype in mind, but this story angle should appeal to your target customers' struggles, fears, hopes, and desires. Think about what they would click on. Consider why they would want to read your story. This is how you select a story angle that uses the archetype approach. Next, select the right outlet that will align with the target customer. What do they read? When? In their spare time? On their phones?

Below are the outlet types that, depending on what industry you are in, tend to offer the highest ROI:

A. *Blog or Website to Fellow Blog or Website Feature or National Digital Platform.*

If you have a blog or website and want to get more traffic, you might consider a fellow blog that isn't exactly the same as yours, but has a similar audience. If you're featured there, they could get excited about you and it will drive traffic to your site. You can also target national platforms like Forbes, Fast Company, or Business Insider to discuss your topic of expertise.

The byline will build awareness and exposure that drives traffic back to your site.

B. *Coach or Course to Top Podcast*

If you are a coach and have a course to sell, you may consider a podcast, where you will have a longer amount of time to talk, share your story, and let the audience build a relationship with you. Since you're a service provider who wants to sell a course, it's important that your audience feels like they can trust you and that you really know your stuff. The conversion on podcasts can be great.

C. *Author to Podcast or Lifestyle Website.*

If you're an author and want to be known as more of a thought leader, you could secure a spot as a guest on a podcast with a reputable host who has a lot of clout in your industry. Or you could work to get yourself featured as an expert on a given topic: like how to overcome burnout, or strategies for work life balance. This could be an outlet like Brit & Co or Hello Giggles or Thrive Global.

D. *Consumer Product to TV or Morning Shows*

If you have a product that people can interact with, TV or morning shows are ideal. They like to have products they can interact with because it makes for more interesting television. They might enjoy a fitness or cooking demonstration, a unique toy, hair product, make-up demonstration, or fashion show.

If you want that cheat sheet, you can download and grab it here (bit.ly/AshleyCheatSheet). My treat.

My goal is to have you achieve maximum results with minimum time and effort. Purposefully plant that one seed to achieve your "breakout story".

It's the leverage you need to get explosive coverage, and see your face and business featured in the outlet of your dreams.

A few pages ago, I told you about the success we got at *Verily* once I picked the perfect angle for our pitch. But how did I get that first breakout story? How did I plant that one seed that helped grow all the others?

I'll tell you.

Before *The Huffington Post* gave us a chance, our breakout story ran in the *New York Post*. An editor for *The Wall Street*

Journal had spoken at an event I attended, and just before the launch, I heard he was speaking at another event and had recently moved to the *New York Post*. I thought it would be great coverage to get the *New York Post* to talk about our magazine, but I'd only seen this editor speak once and we had never met. So, I found him on Facebook and sent him a message prior to the event. I wrote, "I'm so excited to hear your talk. I'm going to be there and I'm excited to meet you." By doing that, I purposefully planted the expectation that he'd see me at the event.

PRO TIP: So many people go into events and they don't maximize the opportunity because the speaker has no idea who they are. Let the speaker know in advance you will be there!

At the event, I listened to him speak, saw some other speakers, and waited carefully. Then, as he was leaving—literally walking out the door—I made a beeline for him. I said, "So great to meet you," and he recognized me! (Because I had sent him a message.) So, I shook his hand and said, "Here's a gift for your wife." I then handed him the magazine. No pitch, no ask. Just the gift, *purposely planted* in his hand.

He read our magazine in his cab on the way home. Days later, we got a call that one of the top editors at the *New York Post* was featuring our story. So, the magazine went out in the *New York Post* in the print issue in a feature called *"What Women Want."*

"That was the seed that grew our press coverage from nothing."

Now, while that seed was growing, I kept paying attention to the other seeds I'd sent out. I wanted to make sure we capitalized on the exposure. So, I created a social campaign from that article about #whatwomenwant, and it started to gain a ton of momentum across social media. While I was monitoring the social channels, I realized people were retweeting the story a lot, so I tracked who was retweeting.

Then one day the VP of all lifestyle programming for Sirius XM Radio retweeted the story. I immediately private-messaged her on Twitter and said, "So excited. Thank you for the support and thank you for the retweet. I would love to talk to you about this. I have so many story ideas to support your community."

And she suggested coffee.

A couple days later, we were at a cozy coffee shop in the West Village with her and the senior producer of all women's programming for Sirius XM. By the end of that conversation, they had offered us the opportunity to produce an entire week of shows on Sirius XM...during New York Fashion Week!

All of a sudden, we went from a print magazine, launching in Barnes & Noble, to also running a series of shows that we could co-produce with guests. From there, the momentum just kept building...and building...and building....

Did you see the movie *The Post* (See page 137), with Tom Hanks and Meryl Streep? In one scene, Streep and Hanks' characters at *The Washington Post* decide to go head to head with the editorial team at *The New York Times* and break a new story at great risk to their publication. That morning, Hanks walks in and dumps out a bag of newspapers that covered the story after *The Washington Post*. Hanks tells Streep, "Not just a neighborhood newspaper now."

That scene captures my entire methodology. Hanks references how *The Washington Post* was regarded as a nondescript neighborhood publication for the DC metro area. But when they broke the feature story and everyone else followed, *The Post* repositioned itself as a power player in the industry. Let this be a lesson for you, also. **When you land major national media attention, all the other smaller publications will get in line to feature you.** It is the fastest method to growing your business because it triggers what I call "The Domino Effect."

The Domino Effect is when every smaller publication falls in line to feature you because they want to appear relevant and respectable like the larger outlets. This means less time, money, or effort on your part, and believe me, **you can leverage that healthy competition to your advantage.**

In our case, I leveraged every initial piece of media coverage so that it snowballed into even more. If I hadn't created the #whatwomenwant social campaign in response to the *New York Post* piece, then Sirius XM may have never seen my story. And if I hadn't followed up on their retweet, I would have never been invited to meet for coffee and could never have suggested producing shows for them during Fashion Week.

You see, the tiniest seeds grow into huge opportunities. And if you know the correct system to follow, they can grow faster than you ever imagined. That's amazing news for every time-starved entrepreneur bootstrapping their business on a small budget. And trust me, these principles will work...even if you have no budget for a PR firm, have never before been featured, are an introvert, have zero tech skills, and are just getting started in business.

So now you know to use story as the hook to get people interested, using archetypes like the Low-to-High and Unexpected Twist examples from *ImageThink* and *Verily.* And you know how to do your homework and pitch the big platforms first, so you create a domino effect, i.e., smaller media outlets picking up your story to stay relevant.

Here is another example of how The Domino Effect works in real life:

DOMINO EFFECT CASE STUDY:

One of my students, Maneesha, is an immigrant who lived in six countries before settling in the United States. She realized how hard it was to immigrate into the US and how much stress and strain it causes people.

Wanting to make a difference and help more people like her, she launched a lawyer-matchmaking platform, Ask Ellis, to help match immigrants with high-quality lawyers to make the process easier than ever before.

But Maneesha felt stuck. She had been in business two years and hadn't received a single feature. She just wasn't seeing the kind of traction she expected. In just a few weeks of working together, her very first feature ever was a full profile in Fast Company.

And then O Magazine reached out to her, and asked to feature her in the September print issue as one of their "trailblazers." Maneesha's website traffic doubled overnight—all because of the system I taught her.

Can you imagine that? *O Magazine* pitching you for the honor of being featured? Now I know what you're saying because a lot of people say it to me: "Ashley, I don't have any connections. How am I supposed to pitch and make connections in the right way when no one knows who I am and I don't know who to talk to?"

I've got a tool for you that's going to save you thousands of dollars on finding those connections, and help you connect with influencers who will cover your brand.

TAKE ACTION:

Decide which outlets you would like to be featured in for your industry. If you would like to use the Media Map Cheat Sheet, again you can get it here: (bit.ly/AshleyCheatSheet).

_____

_____

_____

_____

_____

_____

_____

_____

_____

_____

_____

_____

_____

_____

_____

- -

- -

- -

New Principle #3

Give Before You Get:
Find & Connect with Media Influencers
Without Spending Thousands

PART 1: FINDING INFLUENCERS

E ven if you don't know anyone in the industry, there are some easy ways to plant seeds that can germinate into fruitful relationships. One of the best ways is what we just talked about: sharing valuable stories in your cold pitches positioned with story archetypes. When someone is looking for their next great story, and you hand them one on a silver platter, that makes an amazing first impression. And **first impressions are key to visibility**.

But what if you don't know how to find people to pitch? I'm going to tell you about a FREE tool I discovered in just a second.

First, though, remember to start by thinking about the platforms you'd most like to be published on. What are your dream outlets?

Also think about which platform is best for your particular product or service. For example, TV is great if you have a book or a tangible product to share, but if you're a thought leader or service provider, then a podcast could be best.

Once you know which media platform you'd like to pitch, then you have to find their editor or producer. PR agencies have databases full of contacts, but their monthly retainer costs are quite high. While there are tools that give you access to those contact databases, they can cost upwards of $3,000 per month—which just isn't doable for most business owners at this stage.

Often, media databases are outdated, since there is so much turnover. They are also usually out of reach for small businesses or entrepreneurs due to their cost. So you need the skill set to know how to find the most up-to-date contact information and build relationships that cross over into all platforms.

For example, I pitched a story that went viral to the senior style editor at *The Huffington Post* back in 2013. In 2014, she moved to *Mic.* and offered to let me write a story for them. Now she is at *Racked*, and we still keep in touch. It is about building real relationships.

So before you subscribe to a database service to get someone's contact information, here are ideas on how to find a reporter's contact information:

1. Search the website of the media platform they work for under their personal bio or the "masthead."

2. Look through social media to find them. (I only made contact with the *New York Post* editor who wrote about *Verily* because I found him on Facebook.) Many writers have their contact information listed in their Twitter or LinkedIn bios.

3. You can also find and build great relationships by attending relevant events near you where media influencers are speaking.

There's a tool I want to show you that's going to save you thousands of dollars on database fees. It's a little plugin for Chrome called RocketReach, and it helps you track down the contact info of the people you most need to reach.

The cool thing about RocketReach is that it's free to find five people every month, and it's only $49 per month to jump up to 170 contacts per month. Compared to the cost of a database subscription, that is affordable!

(In case you're wondering, I'm not an affiliate. I just love them and appreciate what they're doing to support entrepreneurs with awesome messages.)

PART 2: CONNECTING

Now you have your story ideas. You're armed with ways to find and contact the people you need to talk to. It is time to package it all in an email that works!!

One of the scary things is writing a pitch that you poured your heart and soul into and then never hearing back. You send it out with all these expectations and its just crickets.

You start to question yourself, it feels personal, you feel rejected, and before you know it, you doubt your whole business idea. I am exaggerating (or maybe not), but what I want to offer you is an email template that works. You can buy them right here (bit.ly/AshleyEmailTemplate). But first, you have to approach this with the right mindset.

If you hear crickets, you just need to follow up. I have a follow-up email script that works time and time again. It's a copy-paste email template you can use to reach out to media and get them to say, "Yes!".

Buy them right here:
(bit.ly/AshleyEmailTemplateDownload).

Remember how I mentioned at the beginning—landing national media attention is not about having a big ego. In fact, to do it effectively, you must have a spirit of generosity. So for now, I have a few final words of advice....

First, always remember to serve people before asking for something from them. I got the story with *The Huffington Post* because I had previously written a viral story for them. This is a method that one of my students used:

SERVE BEFORE ASKING CASE STUDY:

Meet my student, Erin, founder of Hello Divorce. She is a lawyer who wants to streamline the divorce process so that individuals don't have to pay thousands of dollars in order to get a divorce. And she wants to do that through a training program.

But when Erin came to me, she was really nervous because her competition was suddenly being featured everywhere, and she was not. She knew she had a finite amount of time to get featured before her business was toast.

> Within one week of working together, she got an article published in mindbodygreen, a national platform, and soon Brit & Co, Entrepreneur, YourTango, Authority Magazine, Thrive Global, and more came aboard.
>
> How did she do it? She packaged her story into an archetype and pitched an article that she could contribute to their platforms, thereby offering value.

You also have a wealth of knowledge and wisdom to share from your expertise. If you offer to contribute an article to an outlet, you demonstrate value for their platform and begin building a positive relationship that can pay dividends in media features.

Second, remember to leverage any media exposure you receive because it's your best asset for making connections with even more media influencers, just like the #whatwomenwant social campaign that landed me a meeting with Sirius XM Radio.

PRO TIP: Find ways to offer value. You want to build a lasting relationship, so here are seven techniques to make a great first impression with media influencers:

1. Gift them your product at an event or send it to their office.
2. Write a note to let them know how much you enjoy their writing.

3. Follow them on Instagram and comment on their photos.
4. Follow them on Twitter and retweet or share their articles. Writers always want their work to spread as far and wide as possible.
5. Leave them a review on their podcast or book.
6. Offer to bring them coffee at their office in exchange for five minutes of their time.
7. Be genuine.

Those are just a few ways you can make authentic and meaningful connections with media influencers, even if no one has ever heard of you. If you have a great story and you present it in the right way that creates value for the media outlet you're pitching, then people will always be glad to hear from you.

In closing, I want to celebrate you for investing in yourself and your business. Your world opens up when you get out there and pitch yourself to media. By following this roadmap, you can get to the finish line, and get results.

This is your time to level up your visibility and gain exposure, credibility, and positioning before millions of people flood the market and no one knows who is better than the other. Remember, you have a message you were born to contribute.

TAKE ACTION

Who is the first person you will reach out to?
How will you connect with them?
How will you provide value?

_____

_____

_____

_____

_____

_____

_____

_____

_____

_____

_____

_____

_____

_____

_____

_____

_____

_____

_____

Epilogue

Phew, we talked about a lot! Are you excited to start pitching yourself and generate even more momentum for your business? Are you excited to finally start building your "As Seen In" page on your website?

Here is what you learned:

You learned that for maximum impact with minimum time or money, you need to land national media outlets so that you trigger The Domino Effect and smaller outlets start pitching you to be featured.

You learned how to position your story in a way that gets the attention of those national media platforms.

You learned how to find and build relationships with media influencers you can pitch.

Finally, you learned how to leverage any media exposure to have the best chance of turning it into even more features.

It seems like we covered so much, but that is only the outline of the step-by-step system I have built over years of doing this.

I hope you will go out there and start landing the coverage your business deserves, but I know it is hard to do alone. I've seen time and time again business owners—even former PR professionals—who don't know how to structure their pitch letter. Or they take too long to figure things out themselves and they really don't have the time to try to work things out. Or they send some pitches and hear nothing but crickets...in short, they don't know how to create a strategy and media plan that works.

Then there are those people who land some exposure, get the interview, and fall flat because they don't know how to talk about their product or how to act in an interview. Worse still, they don't know how to leverage that interview into more exposure.

If this sounds like you, relax...it's okay. Even if you've had failures, you can always step back and turn it around. And if you're just starting out, you can still get massive results.

CASE STUDY:

My client Kelly is a power player. Former NFL cheerleader turned Fortune 500 executive turned seven-figure business growth strategist, she has a list of accolades too long to count.

Among them is the title "international bestselling author." Kelly came tome because she was launching her second book and wanted to position herself as a premier thought leader in her industry. Until now, Kelly had been on numerous top podcasts, but struggled to break through to get featured on TV.

We created a custom strategy package for her to rework her story angles and a key component: her pitch letters. You see, it all starts with the perfect pitch. Armed with her new story angles and pitch letters, Kelly secured top-brass TV coverage from reputable outlets like ABC, CNBC, and NBC within weeks.

She is now a regular featured expert guest on TV each month, addressing topics such as team building, business growth, and more. She raised her prices by 500% and nobody blinked an eye. This is the power of media positioning. She had many successes before coming to me and a few setbacks. We helped her turn it around and get to the next level.

If you want to stop playing small, land national media attention and position yourself as a power player; if you want a proven step-by-step system that shows you what to do and when, with zero guessing; if you want to learn how to present yourself to the media, how to write a killer pitch letter that gets attention, how to amplify your mission and make a huge impact in the world...

...then I created a program just for you: (bit.ly/AshleyJumpstartProgram).

So from here, you have two options:

You can go it alone and try to do this yourself, struggling and taking time to get things right through trial and error, without the support of an expert who's created incredible results over and over again. Or...

You can invest in me and my system. You can link arms with me as your guide who has been where you are, bypassed the clog, and has the results to prove it.

I can give you a plan that gives you maximum results in minimal time, where you can access the in-depth strategies I used to create success for my clients and students in nine countries.

You can become a Power Player.

Ask advice from people who have done what you want to do. Seek guidance from people who have what you want. If you have a high level of care for growing your business (and if you have read this far, I assume you do), this is your moment to serve at a deeper level with your big work in the world.

But first, let's hear from James Da Costa, a student of mine who said yes to this big work... and you can gauge for yourself whether the results were worth it:

CASE STUDY:

"Before I met Ashley, I talked about my work in a round-about way - whether that was focusing on technical details or sharing facts without a purpose to link them together.

Working with Ashley not only helped me realise I had a story to tell, but made me realise that sharing my story was valuable both to others and my social enterprise.

I already knew my purpose, but Ashley helped me tell it in a way for other people to understand.

Since then, I've become a contributor to Forbes, spoken at UN Global Goals Week, run workshops at the U.K. House of Parliament and was recently awarded to the 2019 Forbes 30 Under 30 list for social entrepreneurship."

If this sounds good to you, I would love to tell you about Master the Media *Jumpstart*. *Jumpstart is a* publicity accelerator that is a proven plan to land your breakout media story in a top platform in 30 days or less.

Jumpstart is designed to set you up for with breakout media stories that will help you go from unknown to unforgettable with a proven plan people are raving about. It includes mentorship and video messages from me, to help you get results like the ones you just read about.

Remember, media is the foundation of your business growth, but you have to do it in the right way.

Jumpstart reverse engineers the PR industry and gives you the best performing plans in a highly detailed, step by step system to land your breakout story so you can position yourself in the right way and scale. No guesswork and no fluff. *Jumpstart* holds your hand throughout the entire process.

How would you like to have a personal guide to mentor you past all the pitfalls right to the results? Now you have it. Think of me as your personal PR agent. With *Jumpstart*, I am lifting that purple velvet rope and inviting you inside the exclusive club of brands and businesses that get huge coverage from some of the most elite publications in the world. With this opportunity, people start seeing results in as little as 24 hours, so believe me when I say, it is incredibly powerful and like nothing on the market today.

If you are interested in going from unknown to unforgettable, stop playing small, and position yourself as a power player, I invite you to join us now.

Why I Created Master the Media *Jumpstart*

Master the Media *Jumpstart* is my agency's playbook. It's the blueprint we use to create outstanding results for our clients since Appleseed's founding.

But last year I realized that the world has changed. More than ever we now live in a sharing economy. And I kept meeting amazing go getters, doing amazing things, who couldn't afford to spend six-figures to work with PR agencies.

I knew there had to be a solution. It didn't feel right to only charge high retainer prices that many people cannot afford, hoard relationships that could benefit everyone, and keep the knowledge to myself.

So, I created Master the Media *Jumpstart*. It reveals everything you need to amplify your message and land major media exposure without a major budget. Step by step it walks you through the exact system I developed for my clients and shows you how to implement the steps in your own business. Ready to go from unknown to unforgettable?

If you are a quick start action taker begging to get in, you can go ahead and enroll right now: bit.ly/AshleyJumpstartProgram

For those who love more research, here are some things to consider: this is how much it would normally cost to work with an agency to cover everything you will receive in Master the Media:

- $5000 monthly payment for media placement and strategy
- $7500 monthly payment for speaking pitching plus media placement
- $10,000+ monthly payment for strategy, positioning rebrand, speaking pitching, media placement, and training.

(These are REAL rates that my clients pay to work with Appleseed.)

When you add up a launch the bill could total $100,000. Premier service at a luxury price tag.

That was a big problem for a lot of people who wanted to work with me... and that's why I designed Master the Media *Jumpstart* for you.

For the solopreneur, the changemaker, the emerging business owner. The person who self-funded their business because they have a dream to help more people. To make a bigger contribution on this planet. This for you. If you're serious about hitting the big time, if you understand the power of amplifying your message and your mission: let me help you.

If you need a system that works from a proven expert to launch your publicity to another level....

If you want to build your audience and community and step forward as a thought leader...

If you're hungry for more significance and impact, with less headaches and hustle...

If you want major media opportunities dropping in your lap via Facebook DM...

This is for you.

It's so important to me that Master the Media *Jumpstart* is accessible to the amazing entrepreneurs out there making their mark and changing the world for good. And I understand that no matter how powerful your vision and your mission: if you haven't managed to amplify those on your own, budgets can be tight.

That is why you need a mentor. But not just any mentor. There are too many coaches cluttering up our social feeds selling unproven methodologies. If you are going to select a guide - whether I am the right one for you or not - ask advice from people who have done want you want to do.

My *Jumpstart* program, the whole step by step system, contains over $15,000 in true value.

But if you enroll in Master the Media *Jumpstart* today, you have only a one-time payment of $497. I don't want anything getting in the way of your goals. This is the ultimate priority you need to take action on. You will never see this price again or anywhere else. This might sound crazy, but my team is instructed never to offer it to anyone. Why? Because it won't work for everyone. It works for action-takers and go getters. Because you just read this entire book, I know that is what you are.

Media rewards the action takers, like you.

But sometimes people hustle for years working on the wrong things and end up exhausted and frustrated. If you are getting stuck in feast or famine, want more clients, more credibility this year, media features are that missing piece you can put in place to rapidly scale your company, close sales faster, and position you in a whole new professional category as the premier Power Player that you are.

The time is now to begin planning your media campaign and position yourself as a premier expert with media, and it's never been easier or more affordable to get started with this *Jumpstart* plan.

If you want to learn the exact system I've used to help my clients and students go viral and land major media coverage, fast: I invite you to invest in yourself and in your business.

If you want the whole system broken down step by step: with templates, scripts, fun sheets, mindset exercises, 13 story archetypes, (Did you like the ones you read about? The rest are inside *Jumpstart*.), my highest performing headlines guaranteed to get your emails read, how to build your expert professional bio, special video messages from me as your personal trainer, 60-day Press Planner, list of outlets to begin pitching immediately, 5 proven pitch templates for only $497 you need to sign up right now.

Claim Jumpstart here: (bit.ly/AshleyJumpstartProgram).

If you are on the fence, consider this: time is not free. Every day that goes by and you don't have these skills, and opportunities pass by, is time that your business is losing money and not reaching as many people, clients, and customers as it could. You are robbing yourself of the exposure, credibility, and positioning that will rocket you into a league of your own so you can drown out your competitors and become a category of one. I would love to change that like I have done for my students.

Congratulations!

You have completed the high-end publicity training in this book. You are now armed and equipped with a proven blueprint that works at the highest levels of media, worldwide. Use this knowledge with great care. For full benefit, get in motion today to implement the lessons so you can see the results. If you are ready, join us inside *Jumpstart* and go from unknown to unforgettable and position yourself as a Power Player.

Jumpstart Program: bit.ly/AshleyJumpstartProgram

Interested in learning more?
Book a free 15-minute
Power Up Assessment with my team
(bit.ly/AshleyPowerSession)
to explore how we can serve you
with one of our custom solutions.

Enjoyed what you just read?
Please take a second to leave a review.

**WRITE A REVIEW
(bit.ly/AshleyBookReview)**

We value any type of feedback from YOU.

Want to connect with other
high achievers ready to raise big publicity?
Join my free community,
Media Masters with Ashley Crouch
(http://bit.ly/PPFBGroup)

APPENDIX

Intuit study on 50% of US workforce will be freelancers by 2020: http://http-download.intuit.com/http.intuit/CMO/intuit/futureofsmallbusiness/intuit_2020_report.pdf

Brian Chesky interview: https://venturebeat.com/2014/07/02/airbnb-ceo-spells-out-the-end-game-for-the-sharing-economy-in-7-quotes/

Ashley Crouch Forbes interview with Ali Brown: https://www.forbes.com/sites/ashleycrouch/2018/10/10/how-to-position-yourself-as-a-premier-expert-ali-brown

The Post movie with Tom Hanks and Meryl Streep: https://www.imdb.com/title/tt6294822/

WORKSHEETS

TAKE ACTION

Remember your why.
If media could help you achieve
Anything in the next six months,
what would that be?

_____

_____

_____

_____

_____

_____

_____

_____

_____

_____

_____

_____

_____

_____

_____

_____

_____

_____

TAKE ACTION:

Of these three, which is your biggest obstacle?
Name it and claim it below.
Once you know the culprit, you can move forward.
In the meantime, here are 3 affirmations to reset
your mind for visibility success:

1. I have a message I was born to contribute.
2. I don't just have a message; I am the message.
3. My story offers value to everyone I meet.

_____

_____

_____

_____

_____

_____

_____

_____

_____

_____

_____

_____

_____

_____

_____

_____

TAKE ACTION

Are you ready to move forward?
Yes or no?

_____

_____

_____

_____

_____

_____

_____

_____

_____

_____

_____

_____

_____

_____

_____

_____

_____

_____

_____

TAKE ACTION:

Decide which outlets you would like to be featured in for your industry. If you would like to use the Media Map Cheat Sheet, again you can get it here: (bit.ly/AshleyCheatSheet).

_____
_____
_____
_____
_____
_____
_____
_____
_____
_____
_____
_____
_____
_____
_____
_____
_____
_____
_____

TAKE ACTION

Which archetype can you use for your business?
Draft three suggested example headlines.

_____

_____

_____

_____

_____

_____

_____

_____

_____

_____

_____

_____

_____

_____

_____

_____

_____

_____

_____

_____

ABOUT THE AUTHOR

Ashley Crouch is an award-winning visibility strategist and the founder of Appleseed Communications, the first "one for one" agency to exist. For every client served, Appleseed offers a micro-loan to a woman entrepreneur in 21 resource-poor nations such as the Philippines, Kenya, Nicaragua, Malawi, and Cambodia.

In 2011, Ashley was on the founding team for the "first no-Photoshop fashion magazine", Verily, and secured 180 media features in eight months, entirely self-taught. The magazine currently receives one million views per month.

Ashley has written for Forbes, The New York Times, Business Insider, Fast Company, TIME.com, The Huffington Post, Refinery29, Bust, and more. She has trained almost two thousand people worldwide on visibility and publicity strategy in the last year.

She speaks on leadership, publicity strategy, and entrepreneurship to audiences at Princeton University, University of Texas at Austin, Altitude Summit, WeWork, DocuSign, SheWorx, United Healthcare, and the Lady Project National Summit.

Ashley and her businesses have been featured in Forbes, American Express, TODAY.com, Brit & Co, The Huffington Post, The Daily Telegraph, International Business Times, SWAAY, Thrive Global. She was a Forbes Under 30 nominee for 2017 in Social Entrepreneurship.

Connect with Ashley on Social Media:

FACEBOOK (bit.ly/AshleySocialMediaFB)

INSTAGRAM (bit.ly/AshleySocialMediaInsta)

LINKEDIN (bit.ly/AshleySocialMediaLinkedin)

WEBSITE (bit.ly/AshleySocialMediaWebsite)